Presented to

Thomas & Donna
April 30, 1978

By

Mother

Growing Together

PRAYERS FOR MARRIED PEOPLE

Leslie and Edith Brandt

AUGSBURG PUBLISHING HOUSE

Minneapolis, Minnesota

GROWING TOGETHER

Copyright © 1975 Augsburg Publishing House

Library of Congress Catalog Card No. 75-2830

International Standard Book No. 0-8066-1476-5

For information address Augsburg Publishing House,
426 South Fifth Street,
Minneapolis, Minnesota 55415.

Manufactured in the United States of America

CONTENTS

This joint project of writing prayers for married people has been an interesting experience for us. Thinking together through some of the joys and conflicts of married life and then attempting to project them through the medium of personal prayers made us realize anew what adventure marriage holds for two people who really want to work at it. We were again reminded that marriage encounters risk of every description. Nevertheless, for the couple who trusts in God for guidance and direction from courtship into retirement and for two people who are intent upon keeping the lines of communication open and their selfishness subdued, marriage really is an exciting adventure. We highly recommend it.

We wanted these prayers to be general enough to express at least some of the concepts that are relevant to most Christian marriages. We hope that you will be able to apply them in some measure to your specific needs and that these prayers will help you find words for expressing your prayer thoughts to God. You may not want to use these prayers exactly as they are written; they may not precisely fit your situation. Adapt them as you like: substitute "wife" for "husband," "son" for "daughter," or masculine pronouns for feminine. Make the prayers your own.

May God bless and prosper your marriage.

BEGINNING

NOW WE'RE MARRIED

We're married, Lord.
We know that marriage is considered
a serious risk, a gamble,
in this day of superficial relationships.
And we know that the ecstatic feelings
and the warm glow that embraces us
in this hour
may not always saturate our marriage.
But we believe our love is real, O Lord,
and our trust in each other is total.
And we are assured that our marriage
is within your will for our lives.
We know, as well,
that we cannot succeed by our efforts alone.
We need your help and even the help of our
concerned families and friends to keep this
a permanent and ever-maturing relationship.
Our commitment to each other must be
controlled by our individual and mutual
commitments to you and your purposes.
If we each choose your path for us, our God,
we will walk together;
and despite the rough spots along the way,
we'll walk in faith and joy.
Grant, O God,
that our marriage may be pleasing to you
and a source of joy and strength to others.

SHE'S MINE, LORD!

Now she's mine, Lord,
and my heart is exploding with gratitude.
I love her more than life itself,
and her love for me has pushed back
the shades of uncertainty
and bathed my future with hope.
You knew that I couldn't go it alone, O God,
and you graciously enveloped my life
with love by way of this one you gave to me.
And yet, she is not mine, Lord.
She belongs to you.
You lovingly share her with me,
not only to show me love,
but to teach me how to love.
Forbid, O Lord, that I seek to possess her
or regard her as my personal property.
And forbid that we become so engrossed
in one another that we neglect
your objectives and purposes for our lives.
Grant, O God, even while I hold her close,
that I may never come between you and her,
but that we inspire and assist each other
in following your course for our lives.
I thank you for my dear wife, O God.
May she find my love for her as comforting
and assuring as is her love for me.
I pray that our relationship will make us
more devoted to you
so that we will glorify and serve you
in the course of our lives together.

HE BELONGS TO ME

He is my husband, O God,
but he really doesn't belong to me.
He is your son and servant
even as I am your child and disciple.
His first call and obedience
is to you and your purposes.
And yet I am grateful that you will permit me
to share his life and his call,
and that we,
together and apart from the other,
may serve you
by serving your children about us.
I cherish my husband, O God.
I pray that he will always cherish me.
Help me, my God, to be the kind of wife
who will strengthen his abilities
and support his obedience to you.
I praise you, my Lord, for your gift to me.
Help me to be worthy of my husband,
and may we, together,
become more effective and useful
as your faithful servants.

I AM LOVED

All the lights in this dark world
are turned on, dear Lord,
because my husband loves me!
I do believe in your divine love,
that you accept me just as I am,
that you will not reject me
even when I fail to please you.
I also have family and friends
who show love and concern for me.
Yet I have often found it difficult
to feel loved, to blot out the loneliness
that closed in about me.
But now I know that I am loved!
In the tender embrace of my mate
I even feel your great love;
I have the assurance that you are near
to accept me just as I am,
to care about me and for me.
I thank you, my loving God,
because you have shared yourself with me
even through this man whom I love.
Help me to reflect and transmit your love
to him that he, too, may feel your nearness
in my tender concern for him.

OURS TO SHARE

We truly love one another, dear Lord,
and we know that our love will grow deeper
now that you have graciously led us into
the blessed union of marriage.
We feel so good about our love
for one another that we can't help
but feel love for others as well.
My this always be so, O God.
Help us to understand that our love
is not ours to keep but ours to share,
and that in our love for one another
we may learn more
about how to love people around us.
Grant that your eternal love for us
and our love for one another
may make us instruments and channels of love
to other people,
and especially to the lonely and unloved
who cross our paths through life.

THANK YOU
FOR ONE ANOTHER

We thank you for one another, Lord.
We thank you for the sometimes imperceptible
leading of your Spirit that made
our meeting and mating a glorious reality.
We know that you brought us together.
We are assured that this is your doing,
and we entrust our relationship
and our lives together into your loving hands.
We know, however, that it won't be easy, Lord.
We are, each of us,
self-centered, opinionated products
of our background and upbringing.
We have much to confess, much to learn,
and much to change
as you mold us into the kind of team
that will effectively serve you
in your course for our lives.
We do, O Lord,
individually and mutually
commit ourselves to you.
Help us to be faithful, Lord,
to you
and to one another.

THE JOURNEY
BEFORE US

We are at the beginning of a new
and wonderful journey, Lord.
We know where we have been—
the sorrows and the joys,
the triumphs and defeats of our past lives.
We do not know what lies ahead.
There will be pitfalls as well as pleasures.
Our hours of happiness will be interrupted
by times of despair.
Mountains will be interspersed with valleys.
The road will sometimes be rough and rutted.
We are grateful, O God,
that we can travel together.
We pray that we may continue
to walk side by side,
supporting one another
and garnering from you and from each other
the grace and strength we need,
discovering in the midst of difficult hours
that deep inner peace and joy of knowing
that we are surrounded
by your loving concern;
and we need never lose our way.
We enlist our lives in your purposes, Lord.
You are our Shepherd, our Captain and Pilot,
our constant companion.
Grant, O God, that we may follow you forever.

SEX IS LIKE
A SACRAMENT

Married love can be beautiful, Lord.
We need to express it verbally
in tender and passionate phrases.
We must learn how to demonstrate it
in action and in deed.
Yet we need so much the touch, the embrace,
the physical act
that draws us into one another
with the gentle and explosive mingling
of our bodies and spirits.
As you have granted the church your very
special touch by way of your sacraments,
to confirm and affirm your eternal love,
so you have granted to marriage a means
by which the love of husband and wife
may be renewed and deepened.
We gratefully accept this precious gift
and we accept the joy, the excitement,
the physical ecstasy,
as well as the spiritual significance
of this privilege and experience.
Grant, O God, that we may be kind
and considerate in every aspect
of our relationship
and that we recognize and use the gifts
you have designed to make our marriage
meaningful and joyful.

MARRIAGE
CAN BE HAZARDOUS

We are aware, our loving God,
that marriage can be hazardous.
The experiences of others about us,
the statistics concerning
marriage and divorce,
are not all that encouraging.
It is, indeed, quite possible
that we will not find the happiness
that we promise ourselves,
that our relationship may curb or limit
personal aspirations or expectations
and may even dissolve
in suffering and tragedy.
Our marriage will not be bathed
in perpetual bliss, O Lord;
but if we allow you to have your way with us,
it can and it will develop and mature
our individual lives and forge us into
a partnership that will bring us much joy
in serving you and in living
within your plan for our lives.
So be it, Lord.
Make your objectives primary for us.
And help us to draw from you the grace
to love one another
and to project genuine love
for the human family about us.

CHILDREARING

DO WE REALLY
WANT CHILDREN?

Our dear Lord, we are apprehensive about
the prospect of having children in our kind of world.
We do want them, but the risk is so great
that we sometimes feel we could better
serve you if we dedicated our efforts
and energies toward helping others
within the human family about us.
Should we rather give serious consideration
to adopting some homeless child
or to giving aid for the unwanted youngsters
in our community?
Maybe our motives are selfish—
and we are seeking to evade
the responsibility or we fear the consequences
of rearing our own children
in an environment that appears to be
increasingly hostile to family-life.
Perhaps we would rather not be tied down
to those tasks that may limit our freedom.
You have, O God, graciously and precariously
left the ultimate decisions in our hands.
We truly want to do your will.
Remove from us the doubts, the fears,
and those self-centered aspirations
that should have no place in our lives.
Enable us to determine your heart's desire
and to make our decision in accordance
with your will and objectives.

A BABY ON THE WAY

A baby is on the way, Lord,
and our hearts are filled
with ever-increasing delight
as we marvel at the awesome mystery
of being cocreators with you.
We are grateful for this blessed privilege.
Even while we parents-to-be rejoice
in being the recipients of your love
and the instruments of your will,
we regard with apprehension
this responsibility that is ours.
We feel so much
the need of relating more deeply to you.
We look forward with expectancy and joy
to the birth of our child.
As we cling more closely to one another,
we commit ourselves to you
resting in the confidence
that this baby is in your embrace,
that you will care for our child and for us.
We pray that each of us and our child may be
your children
and your beloved servants forever.

A MOST PRECIOUS GIFT

You have presented to us
a lovely child, O God, and our hearts
are almost exploding with gratitude.
You have blessed us with a wonder-filled
token of your love for us
and of your trust in us as your servants.
Grant to us, loving Lord,
the grace to believe that with this gift
are also given the strength and the wisdom
to faithfully carry out our responsibility.
This delightful creature
is your child, O God.
We are privileged to enjoy her
and commissioned to share our lives with her.
Accept our thanksgiving
for this beautiful gift, our Lord.
We willingly receive the joys and the sorrows,
the comfort and the pain,
that accompany the gift of this child.
We dedicate ourselves
to bringing her up as your child
and pray that she may love and serve you always.

A FRIGHTENING
AND BLESSED RESPONSIBILITY

O God, it is a frightening responsibility
to assume the task of rearing our children.
It is with fear and trembling
that we accept this awesome charge,
trusting that with this responsibility
is also granted the grace we so much need
to meet this challenge successfully.
It is also a blessed and important calling,
and we are amazed and gratified that you
chose to entrust us with it.
We know we are neither worthy nor qualified,
but we must believe that you will be with us
and help us,
and somehow through us work out
your purposes with our young ones.
As we will be enriched through the lives
of these children,
so grant that they may be made rich
in love and joy
by way of your Spirit
through us.

FOR THOSE
WHO TEACH OUR CHILDREN

O Lord, there are so many things
that we cannot do for our children.
We must often entrust them
to the care of others,
those with special talents and training.
Most important, next to their parents,
are their teachers.
We thank you, our loving God,
for those who teach our children.
Give them joy as they pursue the arduous
and often thankless task
of exposing young minds to the wonders
of heaven and earth
and to the complex problems
of living in this world.
We pray for these teachers of our youth.
Grant them the strength, the patience,
and the wisdom that they need to carry
out their all-important responsibilities.
Help them to love their charges and to find
challenge and excitement in teaching them.
We pray, O Lord, that they may enjoy
some of the benefits of their loving service
to our children as they assist us
in preparing them for service
in your eternal kingdom.

ENTRUSTING THEM TO GOD

We know, O God,
that we have been made responsible
for our children,
that you expect us to be faithful
as their parents and protectors.
It is a task beyond our abilities,
and we need your special grace to do
the job we have been commissioned to do.
And we know, our Lord,
that no matter how hard we try,
our children do not always follow the course
that we have laid out for them.
We can only do what we thought we had done,
entrust them to you.
You know their inner hearts far better
than we, O God.
Even when they turn from you,
you will never give them up.
Pursue them, O God, stay close to them;
draw them back to yourself and your will
for their lives.
We claim your forgiveness for our failures,
O Lord, and place these dear ones
in your loving care.
We pray that the paths they travel,
even if they lead through the waste lands
of darkness and despair,
may ultimately lead them back to you
and to the light and joy of your purposes
for their lives.

LOVING AND SPANKING

Our children are so rebellious
and disobedient at times, our Lord,
that we find it almost impossible
to deal with them.
We want them to feel our love,
yet we become so angry
that we are sometimes unreasonable
in our attempts to discipline them.
Teach us, O God,
how to be wise and mature parents.
Help us discover how to be truly loving
even in our anger,
and to agree together as parents on the kind
of discipline that will bring our children
into mature and reasonable relationships
with us and their peers.
Our primary responsibility, O Lord,
is to communicate your love
by way of our love for them.
Teach us how to love them genuinely—
not permissively—
and may it be the kind of love
that they can understand and believe in
even when they are disciplined.
Help us, O God,
to be faithful and wise stewards
in the rearing of our children.

THE DISTANCE
BETWEEN US

Our loving Lord,
we are disturbed by the distance, the void,
that seems to exist between us and our children.
Once so attached to us, so dependent on us,
they now seem to be just using us
to shelter and clothe them while they
pursue their own questionable activities.
We feel unneeded at times, even unwanted.
Their goals and aspirations—
if they have any at all—
are so different from what we tried to teach them.
Are we, perhaps, guilty of widening this gap?
We cannot condone all their thinking and doing,
but neither should we ridicule
their philosophies and objectives.
Enable us to listen to their ideas
and to love and accept them in spite of
their moral lapses and hang-ups,
entrusting them to you and your guidance.
Help us, O God, to narrow the gap between us,
to love our children even when it means
allowing them the freedom to make
questionable choices and decisions.
Grant, O Lord,
that our love may be the kind that they can feel
and will return to if the road they travel
becomes difficult or impassable.

A PROBLEM CHILD

We are, O God, the parents of a child
who is of very special concern to us.
He's not like most other children that we know.
We become, at times,
anxious and disturbed about our inability
to relate to him and communicate with him,
to be the kind of parents that he needs
at this time in his life.
We love our child; he is your gift to us.
We believe that he is your child,
that we are assigned the important position
of being his guardians and teachers.
Yet we are so often frustrated
by our inability to know and to do
what is right and best for him.
Help us, O God, to love him as you love him,
and grant that he may sense that love
in our stumbling efforts to care for him.
Give us the patience to love him
in our years together
and the grace to share his burdens and hurts.
Guide him along your path for him.
Bless him, our Lord,
and may he be your child
and your servant forever.

LISTENING
TO OUR CHILDREN

It is so easy, O Lord,
to tell our children what they ought to be
or what they ought to do.
We often forget that they are real people,
with real feelings and fears, desires and ambitions.
Rather than seek to understand them,
we attempt to program them,
insisting that they conform to our image,
trying to mold them into replicas of ourselves.
They are at times so lovely,
at times so cantankerous,
but they are your children, Lord,
filled with your Spirit.
We want so much that they develop
and mature in accordance with
your will and plan for their lives.
Teach us, to treat them like persons,
even while we must lovingly discipline them,
to listen to them—their childish explosions
of anger and frustration, their doubts,
fears, joys, and pains—
even to share with them our feelings,
our joys and frustrations,
that they may know that we are all
your human and fallible children.
Help us to truly love our children,
and grant that they may feel
and may be assured of that love.

A PRODIGAL SON

O God, our son has run away.
That one who once trusted us, listened to us
and delighted us, has left us.
We tried hard to rear him in the right way.
We thought we had done everything possible
to give to him the best that we are and possess.
O God, the pain of his leaving us
is almost more than we can bear.
It makes us feel like failures as parents.
We love him—
and now he has shunned our love
and gone his own way.
We no longer feel angry, Lord,
just empty and frightened.
A part of us went with him,
and our prayers and our love
will follow him wherever he goes.
You know him,
his doubts and conflicts, O Lord.
You know where he is—where he is going.
Stay close to him, our God, watch over him.
Bring him back to us, Lord,
but more important, bring him back
into your orbit for his life.
Give to us, O God,
the grace to wait patiently and prayerfully
for our son until the memory of our love
draws him back to us once more.

MATURING

We belong together, Lord,
and we want to live together.
We are more important to each other
than we are to anyone else.
Our home, our table, our bed,
the larger part of our joys and sorrows—
they are ours together.
Yet let there be spaces between
our togetherness, Lord.
While we are closer to each other
than we are to any other human being,
keep us from being so close
as to obscure one another,
to stand in the way of the other,
to stifle or shroud the uniqueness,
the personality, the aspirations,
the talents and capabilities,
even the ambitions and goals that are
the possessions of each of us as individuals.
Teach us how to share, dear Lord,
because only as we remain individuals will we
be able to share what we are and have;
but forbid, O God,
that we stand in the shadow of the other.
Help us to make our mutual,
and our distinctly individual, contributions
to the accomplishment of your purposes.

WHEN PETTINESS POLLUTES

I know it's silly, Lord,
when I allow petty things such as
my husband's mannerisms
or personality differences
to endanger the possibility
of an open and loving relationship.
Give me strength, Lord,
and patience,
and help me to understand
that there is no creature in all the world
that could perfectly fulfill
my almighty prescriptions
and impossible dreams for a mate.
Help me, dear Lord,
to handle the little things
that come between us
so I may have the energy and the will
to contribute to the greater
and more important aspects
of our relationship.
Above all, help me to be a true lover
even when these little things
get in the way.

WHEN HE IS DEPRESSED

Forbid, O God, that I be so tied to my mate
that I must always share his gloom.
Today, Lord, he is flattened by despair,
and I don't want to be part of that scene.
Rather than flounder with him
in the muck of depression,
help me to infiltrate his despondency
and darkness with joy and light,
to be genuinely calm and cheerful.
I know that I must not ignore him
or be indifferent to his pains and problems.
Neither should I commiserate with him
and thereby accentuate his unhappiness.
Grant me the wisdom to be helpful
in encouraging him to focus on you
rather than on negative circumstances.
I ask for the grace to respond to his problem
with love
that will subtly bring him back
to conscious joy once more.
Whatever the reason for his misery,
help me to be patient and understanding.

DIFFICULT WORDS TO SAY

I can mouth many words on many subjects, Lord,
but the hardest words of all are the words,
"I am wrong, and I am sorry."
It is easier to say them to you, O God,
than it is to my loving spouse.
I know that it is because of my pride,
my determination to be better than
others about me.
I am afraid of honesty and openness,
afraid that my balloon may be punctured,
my ego deflated.
Help me, O God, to break through the stupid,
self-righteous barriers
I unwittingly erect about myself
and to dare to be candid and honest.
Teach me, my Lord,
that while I must be cautious
about those revelations of wrong-doing
that may cause others pain,
I must be willing to take the risk
of admitting my failures
and accepting responsibility for my errors.
Grant to me the courage to say,
"I am wrong."

INFIDELITIES

We realize, O God,
that there is not only the possibility
of some gross act of unfaithfulness
that poses a threat to our marriage,
but the probability of many little
infidelities that permeate our relationship.
We are so often unfaithful to one another.
There are the sins
of commission and omission,
of taking too much and giving too little.
We are still basically
and basely self-centered.
We grapple for whatever will satiate
our personal needs
but often fail to consider
and fulfill the needs of the other.
Forgive us, O Lord, for holding back what we,
by your grace,
are capable of giving.
Teach us how to give generously and sacrificially
of ourselves to each other.
And forbid, O God, that we seek to extract
from the other those things
that one is not able to grant.
Help us to be faithful to one another.

TOTAL FREEDOM
FOR TOTAL LOVING

You are, our great God, the loving liberator.
You have set us free from the nagging demon of guilt,
even the haunting memories
of past errors and foolish mistakes.
We don't have to be selfish, jealous,
possessive creatures, afraid of losing
each other's love and affection.
Your grace has set us free to love—
to love one another totally—
and to extend your love to other people.
We know, O Lord,
that we fail to claim and to live up
to that freedom that is ours.
We are often tied to our own self-centered
notions of what we are or ought to be.
We continue to scramble for accolades,
trying to feel successful and significant.
Thus we are more often involved
in self-seeking than in serving,
and our contributions to the world about us
are stifled.
Enable us, O Lord,
to realize our freedom and to experience
the joy of living within that freedom,
the freedom to love totally
and serve sacrificially
within the human family about us.

VOCATION
AND AVOCATION

Teach us, our loving God,
how to put first things first,
how to make you and your objectives
the most important goal of our lives.
We are so very important to one another.
Our children and their welfare are more dear
to us than life itself.
Most of the hours of each day
are allocated to feeding and clothing
ourselves and our family.
And yet these things do not constitute
our central vocation, our reason for living.
You are our Lord and our Master.
Our vocation is focused on you and your will.
Everything else about us is subservient
to your will and design for our lives.
And this is true in respect to
each of us as individuals
as well as to our family relationships.
Help us, O Lord,
to keep our loyalties and allegiances
in the proper order
and to discover that true joy is found
only in a faithful and obedient relationship
to you.

TOO TIRED TO TOUCH

There are times, our Lord,
because of the frustrations of the hour
or the pressures of our daily duties,
that we are too tired to touch one another,
too weary to take the time
for loving embraces.
Or it may be the consequence of fear
or misunderstanding,
the feeling of inferiority,
a sense of inadequacy,
the pain of being hurt or neglected,
the failure to communicate in our
daytime activities,
that makes it difficult,
if not sometimes impossible,
to express our love in joyous consummation.
You have given to each of us
a most wonderful gift.
This embrace of love is of inestimable value
to our relationship.
Forbid, O Lord, that we neglect it
or that we fail to comprehend
one another's sexual needs.
Grant that we may discover our
personal fulfillment in seeking to meet
the needs of our partner as well as our own
and that we will experience mutual joy
in the act of physical embrace.

TEACH US
HOW TO LAUGH

Surely you must be amused
over some of the foolish things
we do, O Lord.
Teach us how to laugh at ourselves—
at some of the petty things
that come between us.
There would be less anger or agony
if there were more laughter,
if we took some things less seriously
and learned how to tolerate
the slip of the tongue
or the slight misunderstanding,
even the little faults and failings,
the oddities and idiocyncrasies
of one another.
Make our laughter
the laughter of love
that becomes a hymn of thanksgiving and praise
to you who have made
our love ever more real
and our relationship ever more meaningful.

STRUGGLING

WHEN THE BURDENS
ARE HEAVY

Sometimes I feel
that I just can't do it, Lord.
I am buried with the burdens
and responsibilities of being both wife
and mother and want so desperately
to run away from it all.
I am ashamed when I turn sour and begin
to take my frustrations out on my family.
Forgive me, Lord,
but I can't seem to help myself.
I know the answer is not in running away.
Is it in you, O Lord,
and in my relationship to you?
Maybe my family expects too much of me,
or I expect too much of myself?
Maybe I'm not really trusting you
or am not open to the grace and strength
that you promise.
I have often prayed for your help, O God.
Enable me to believe that I have it,
and to act as if I have it
when I am unnerved and distressed.
Help me to realize that you love me
and accept me even when so many things
seem to go wrong.

WHEN WE GET
IN ONE ANOTHER'S WAY

There are occasions, O God,
in our demands on the other's time and energy,
when we get in one another's way.
We would never choose to come between you
and the one we love.
We sometimes are so overcome
by our personal needs and problems
that we fail to consider our loved one
and how much that one needs
the perpetual inflow
of your love and peace.
Deliver us, O God,
from incessant self-concern,
our persistent need for the attention
and support of the other.
Teach us how to rely on your grace
and by that grace
to touch one another
with joy and strength and comfort.

LEECH
OR LOVER?

O God, I have often been
more of a leech than a lover.
I have expected more of my wife
than I had any right to expect.
I have exploited her,
used her,
sometimes abused her
in my attempt to extract from her
more than any human being could possibly give
in order to nourish my ego
and support my selfish concerns.
Is it possible
that in my efforts to appear
so helpful and considerate to others,
I have cheated my mate
of the love and concern
that is due her?
O Lord, I know I cannot meet all her needs,
nor can she meet all of mine;
but help me to give more of myself to her,
to cease demanding the impossible from her.
Grant that we may seek from you
the grace and the strength
to live joyfully together
and to contribute effectively
to the needs of men and women about us.

GIVE ME STRENGTH

I know I love him, God,
but sometimes I don't like him very much.
He's so absorbed in his own little world,
so involved with other people
that he hardly knows that I exist.
I know that he's trying to do his job,
and he believes that by serving others
he is truly serving you.
But I feel neglected, Lord—left out.
I want to be loved, too, to be courted,
the object of some concern and consideration.
I must trust, O God,
that you will deal with my husband.
He is your problem even more than he is mine.
I know that I am sometimes selfish
and impatient,
that I may expect too much from him.
Forgive my complaint, dear Lord,
and give me strength.
Help me to accept from you,
in whatever ways you choose to grant them,
the things I need that he cannot provide.
Make me, O God,
a loving, giving, sharing, and caring person,
and help me to entrust
my husband's weaknesses and strengths,
his good traits and his bad,
into your all-knowing and grace-giving hands.

WHY ARE WE
SO DIFFERENT?

You made us from different molds, Lord.
Sometimes we think we are not at all alike.
This was not so obvious
before we were married.
We enjoyed talking and thinking
about the same things.
Our goals, desires, ambitions
followed the same course.
It hasn't always worked out that way
throughout the years.
Are we changing, Lord?
Are we pulling away from each other?
Forbid, O God, that our differences
should come between us.
Grant to us the grace to be grateful
for the other's gifts and convictions.
Help us that we may support one another
and through our love and concern
challenge and enrich
those valid and worthwhile differences
that make each of us unique.
May we, O God, through our commitment to you
and our love and respect for each other,
be drawn together
into an ever-growing and maturing relationship.
Thank you, Lord,
even for our differences.

WHEN I CAN'T
REACH HIM

O God, he's so distant and aloof today,
this husband of mine.
Someone significant
must have patted him on the back
and put him up there
where I can't reach him.
Or maybe he has been successful
in some project or other
and is relishing the sweet smell of victory.
I guess I'm jealous, Lord,
and I'm tempted to tumble him
from his high position
and bring him down to my size.
I find it much easier
to nurse him in his despair
than to share in his exultation.
Maybe that says something about me
and my foolish feelings of self-worth.
Teach me, dear Lord,
how to assess and accept myself
that I may rejoice with him
and share in his successes,
as well as to love and comfort him
in his failures.

THOSE WORDS THAT KILL

Not only can sticks and stones
destroy a loving relationship
but also loaded words
like *always* and *never*.
We don't really mean them
when we act or react in anger toward one another.
They just happen, they spill out—
these words—
and they hurt terribly
someone that we love
and a relationship that is important to us.
The tongue can, indeed,
be an instrument of destruction
if it is not controlled by you, O Lord.
Teach us how to speak softly, O God,
and rationally and fairly,
even when we are angry.
Forgive us for hurting one another.
Make our tongues the bearers
of comfort and encouragement.
And whether our anger is well-founded or foolish,
give us the grace
that leads to a deeper walk with you
and a more mature love for one another.

HELP HER TO CATCH UP

O Lord, I feel very lonely
in this course you would have me take.
Not only do my friends fail to support me,
but my very own wife is lagging far behind.
I feel sure that you are speaking to me
about your will in this matter;
can you not also speak to her?
Help her to catch up, Lord.
Enable her to identify with me
in your will for my life
that we may strengthen and encourage
one another
in our pursuit of your objectives.
Or help me to slow down, O Lord.
Maybe she is more sensitive to your leading
than I am,
and it is your restraining hand
on my zealous and overambitious spirit.
Grant me the grace
to be a listener and a learner,
to recognize your speaking and guiding
even through my beloved
whom you have granted to walk and struggle,
suffer and rejoice, with me
on your course for our lives.

We pray, our loving Father,
in the prayer that Jesus taught us,
that you "give us this day our daily bread."
And yet we are not satisfied
with the granting of our necessities.
We are discovering that "cake,"
the soft luxuries of this life,
is inordinately important to us.
Thus we sometimes find our values shifting.
Our relationship to you and to each other
become cluttered with the gimmicks and gadgets
that promise comfort and convenience—
but only obscure
matters that are of eternal significance.
You have promised to fulfill
our needs, our God.
Teach us how to be satisfied with bread,
to be set free from the tyranny of things,
to love wholly,
to serve sacrificially,
and to find our joy in you
and your objectives for our lives.
We thank you, Lord, for our daily bread.

TAKE OVER
AND LOVE HIM FOR ME

I just don't feel much
like loving today, Lord.
I just want to take off for a while,
and be by myself.
Take over, Lord,
and love him a little more for me.
I know that this storm will pass
and the sun will shine again.
I know that I'm feeling sorry for myself,
that I want something from my mate
that he is not always able to give.
I also know
that I probably couldn't find it
in anyone else either,
that I must discover in you the sufficiency
that no human can offer.
Forgive me, O God, for this darkness
that I have allowed to afflict my spirit.
Grant to both of us those things
that we are not capable of giving
to one another.

WHEN FINANCES FRUSTRATE

We become frustrated and fearful, O God,
when we can't make ends meet,
when our outgo threatens
to surpass our income.
We have already learned that we
can't have everything we want.
Now it appears that we may have to forego
some of the things we have always assumed
that we needed.
Even while we must make some sensible
preparations for the future,
teach us how to live one day at a time,
to seek first your kingdom,
and to worry less
about what may happen tomorrow.
You have promised to care for us, O God.
Help us to trust in your promises
and to discover,
even in these disagreeable circumstances
that threaten us,
the importance of walking with you
and of dedicating our lives to your objectives.
Teach us, our Lord,
how to be good stewards of those gifts
that you have placed in our hands,
and how to find our joy in you
regardless of the financial difficulties
that come our way.

SUFFERING

WHEN SHE IS ILL

I love her so much, dear Lord,
that I wish I could take her place
on her bed of pain.
I am so much a part of her
that when she hurts, I hurt.
While I pray for your touch of healing
on her body,
I pray, as well,
for the patience and tenderness,
the love and assurance,
that will bring her comfort and peace
even in her sufferings.
Help me to be strong and understanding,
and grant that, together,
we will trust you to carry out your purposes
even through this illness
that presently shadows our happiness
and tempts us to be anxious and afraid.
I commit her into your loving hands, my God.
Restore her to health and wholeness again.

THE ILLNESS
OF A CHILD

Somehow, our loving God,
all of our disagreements and differences
seem to disappear as we pray together
for the healing of our beloved child.
We are fearful of submitting to your will
if it means the loss of this one
who is so dear to us.
We honestly do not see how we could find
any joy or purpose in life
apart from our child's continued
love and laughter.
And yet this little one is as important
to you as he is to us.
Truly, he is your child—your gift to us—
and we can entrust him to you and believe
that your will shall come to pass.
This we do, O Lord,
and while we pray and hope for his healing,
we pray for the grace to accept
your loving will
which is always good and right
even when it is beyond our understanding.

THE LOSS
OF A CHILD

You gave to us the most beautiful gift
we have ever known, O God,
and then you took it away.
There are moments
when we wish we had never known
the joy of this amazing gift,
this lovely child you entrusted to our care.
Maybe we were not worthy, God,
or faithful stewards of this charge
that you placed in our hands.
There are moments of bitterness, God,
when we are tempted to accuse you of cruelty,
when we dare to doubt
your concern and your love.
And yet we believe you are a gentle Father
who forgives our yesterdays
and blesses our tomorrows and who knows
the pain you permit us to endure today.
We can only pray that you will enable us
to feel what we know we ought to express—
gratitude for the short time that
your gift was entrusted to us,
for the supreme happiness
that was ours together.
You have taken our child, O Lord.
Only you know the reason.
We thank you because we know
he is yours forever.

THE PASSING
OF A PARENT

We knew it had to happen eventually, O Lord.
Nevertheless, it hurts when someone
who was so important to us
is suddenly taken away.
Maybe we regret it all the more because,
in our pursuit of our own goals
and in our fulfillment of each other's needs,
we have neglected our parents—
these great people who made it possible
for all these good things to happen to us.
We thank you for our parents
who have contributed so much to our lives.
Even while we feel sorrow at their absence,
we would not wish that they be held back
from the beauty and glory
you have in store for them.
Our eventual exodus from this world
is assured, O Lord.
Use this experience to deepen our commitment
to your will for our lives
and lead us
in a fearless confrontation
with our ultimate passing from this world
into your eternal domain.
We commend our loved one
to your tender care, O Lord.
He is yours forever.

THE THREAT
OF SEPARATION

Our loving God,
we have come to that point in our relationship
when nothing seems to work,
when it appears right and reasonable for us
to go our separate ways.
We've honestly tried to make it together.
We continue to have feelings
of deep concern for each other.
Perhaps, if we are apart for awhile,
we will more quickly find within ourselves
those things that stand between us—
that make our relationship joyless and painful.
We know, O God, that this is a part of
the sickness that infects our society
and that it lies within each of us.
Somehow we haven't laid hold of your love
and allowed it to heal our wounds
and bring wholeness to our spirits.
We pray, O God, that your miracle-working
grace will put us together again.
Show us how to love one another,
how to accept and respect and honor
each other as individuals.
Give to us the courage to try again,
and this time to be open and honest with you
and with each other
that we may find and follow
your will for our lives.

WHEN ONE
HURTS THE OTHER

We are fragile, Lord;
we break so easily.
We often act like spoiled children
still reaching for personhood or identity.
Each of us insists on his own way—
and expects the other to subscribe to
his own imperfections.
We react in frustration and anger
when one or the other
is not always generous
and kind and understanding.
Thus we hurt each other,
and the day is wasted
in pouting and self-pity.
Forgive us, Lord, and teach us
how to forgive one another quickly.
Heal these foolish hurts we cause one another.
Rid us of these selfish distortions
that threaten our relationship.
Restore us to your loving heart
and immerse us in that divine love
that is total and perfect.

WHEN HUSBAND
LOSES HIS JOB

We claim to believe your promises, O God,
and realize that our dependence
must be on you.
But now the rug has been
pulled out from under us,
and we are frightened by the prospect
of not being able to pay our bills
or care for our children.
We tend to take for granted the good things
that come our way—
even to the point of neglecting you
and failing to walk in your path.
Now, God, we are driven back to you again.
We have no one else to turn to, or lean on.
We pray that your will be done with us.
And help us, our God,
to believe that you will answer our prayer,
that this apparent loss will somehow fit
into your design for our lives.
Restore our confidence in you, Lord.
Help us to believe
that you will continue to fulfill
your promises to care for us,
that you will stay close to us
in these anxious moments.

THE HANDICAPPED BREADWINNER

I have been incapacitated, my Lord.
I can no longer do what I was trained to do
or care for those for whom I am responsible.
I am disturbed and depressed,
anxious and afraid.
I do not know how the needs of my family
will be met,
or how my life can be of any use to you
or to others.
You have promised, God,
never to leave us in our despair,
that you are with us in the midst
of life's tempests and trials.
How I need you now, God!
Help me to sense your loving presence
and the grace I so much need
to keep my balance in this difficult time.
Give to my wife and to me the courage
to hang on and the faith to believe
that you can turn even this tragic event
into something useful and productive.
Make this agonizing experience a blessing
that will purge and renew us.
We thank you, our Lord, that we can commit our
lives and our misfortunes into your hands,
that we are your children
and no one and nothing can come between us
and your love for us.

WHEN WE ARE BORED
WITH ONE ANOTHER

Lord, it seems that the flame
needs to be rekindled.
The sparkle appears to have gone out
of our relationship.
At least the fire is burning very low, O God,
and we need your special touch on our lives.
Maybe it's the glamor that has gone,
the excitement we once felt when
we held each other close.
Maybe we have been so childishly dependent on
ecstatic feelings to shore up our relationship
that when they cool down
we assume love is lost,
and we begin to get bored with one another.
Perhaps we expect too much from the other
rather than sharing
what we are and have with one another.
Help us to be less concerned about
our personal needs and more committed
to serve you through our service to others.
Lead us, together, to seek our joy from you,
the Giver of true and eternal joy,
by concentrating on your objectives
for our lives.
Turn up the fire within us, dear God,
that our lives and our relationship
may glow again and the lives of others
may be warmed and blessed through us.

RELATING

THE NEED FOR FRIENDS

We have each other, Lord,
and we are grateful;
but we also need others to make our lives
rich and fruitful.
Forbid that we become so absorbed
in our own relationship
that we neglect
to extend our love to others
and to receive from them the love
that will enrich and enhance our lives.
Help us to find the kind of friends
who will increase the joy of our marriage;
may we also be to them friends who will
contribute to the strengthening
of their marital relationships.
Then we will be able to help each other
become the kind of families
that will bless and strengthen our communities
and provide a measure of stability
to our great nation.
We thank you for our friends, dear Lord,
our sisters and brothers in Christ,
for we are all members of your family
and are your sons and daughters forever.

CONCERN
FOR OUR CHILDREN

We are worried about our children, Lord.
They seem at times to be rebellious
and indifferent to you and your purposes.
We can't help but feel that we are to blame
when they take off on their precarious journeys
and flirt with those demons of darkness
that are capable of destroying their souls.
We know, O God, that our love for them
cannot coerce them into goodness
any more than your divine and eternal love
can compel us to follow you.
Maybe we are too absorbed in our own failures
and embarrassed by our inability
to lead them aright.
Perhaps our love is selfish—
that we don't love them enough to let them go
even if we can't hold them back.
Help us, O God,
to love them as you love us,
patiently and perpetually,
whatever their decisions and actions.
And, though we cannot program their lives
to fit into our agenda for them,
help us to live in a way
that will lovingly influence them
and eventually draw them back to you.

OUR DAUGHTER
IS GETTING MARRIED

She is your wonderful gift to us, O Lord,
this lovely daughter of ours,
our pride, our joy, our precious possession.
She illuminated our dark nights
and brightened our difficult days.
She helped to make our marriage
meaningful and worthwhile.
Even when we were at odds with one another,
we were united in our love for her.
We know our love is often selfish,
for there is pain intermixed with joy
as we think of her leaving our family
to share her life and beauty with another.
And yet we are more concerned
about her happiness
than our foolish feelings of loneliness,
and we pray for your blessing
upon her marriage with the man she loves.
Grant them much joy, O God.
Watch over them and keep them,
and may the fruits of their marriage
bring as much happiness to them as we have
received through our children.

LEARNING
HOW TO FORGIVE

Our loving Lord,
you have restored us to yourself
through the experience of forgiveness;
now teach us how to forgive one another.
We proclaim to each other our love,
but such proclamations
are hollow and empty
unless we learn how to forgive.
We claim to accept your forgiving love,
yet we are reluctant to accept one another
and are intolerant
of each other's faults and failings.
We have caused one another much pain.
Rather than forgiving,
making up, and starting over,
we crawl into our corners of self-pity
and mope about
like foolish, spoiled children.
We know, O Lord,
that there is no reason
or real love in such antics—
only pride, hurt feelings, and bruised egos.
May our love for one another
resemble your love for each of us.
Help us to say, "I am sorry,"
and to embrace one another in forgiving love.

INLAWS
OR OUTLAWS

We are not always on good terms
with our parents, O Lord.
Sometimes we resent their intrusions
into our lives and affairs,
their obvious attempts
to influence or guide our destinies.
Help us to understand
that they need our love and concern,
and that, in their sometimes distorted ways,
they are demonstrating their love
and concern for us.
Even if we can't understand them, O God,
enable us to tolerate their intrusions,
to put the best possible
interpretation on them,
and to follow your course for our lives
and do what we know is necessary
for our relationship,
regardless of their loving interference.
We still need them
even as they need us.
Forgive us for selfishly
clinging to one another
to the point of excluding them and others
who need our love and attention.

PRIMARY
BUT NOT EXCLUSIVE

We know, O Lord,
that within the human family
our relationship to one another
must be primary.
We are to share, even as one,
your gifts, your life, and your purposes,
as well as our sorrows and joys.
But forbid, O God,
that our relationship be so exclusive,
that we crowd out or neglect our responsibilities
to others who love us
and who need to be loved by us.
Enlarge our capacity to love, O Lord.
While we meet so many of one another's needs,
some of our needs must be met by others.
And there are those to whom each of us may transmit
joy and strength and healing
through our caring and loving.
We pray that our love for one another
may stretch our souls
and give us a greater capacity
to love others.

HOLDING BACK
FROM THE OTHER

Help us, O Lord, to grant to one another
the right to keep things from the other.
Because we are individuals,
there may be matters
in our relationship with you—
and even with others about us—
that we cannot share with that one
whom we love most of all.
Forbid, O God,
that we seek to possess or dominate
the thoughts and feelings
and secret desires of one another.
Yet help us to share gladly,
whatever the cost or the consequences,
those matters that will bless the other
and benefit our husband-and-wife relationship.
And may we share deeply, Lord,
even our very lives,
that our enriched marriage may communicate
to others about us
the joy of living through loving.

LISTENING
TO ONE ANOTHER

As we must listen to you
if we are to hear you speak through your Word
and through your children about us,
so we must learn how to listen
to one another.
Teach us the art of communication
and the discipline of turning off
our self-centered speaking and seeking
to hear what the other has to say.
As we continue to regard
one another as important,
help us regard and respect the importance
of each other's thoughts and feelings.
Make us sensitive to the other
that we may learn,
without verbal expressions,
the conflicts and needs, hurts and fears,
the delights and joys of one another.
Help us to feel, and to listen, O God,
with loving hearts and attentive minds,
to the desires and complaints
of our beloved mates.

THINGS MORE IMPORTANT
THAN MARRIAGE

We need to be reminded
from time to time, Lord,
that there are things in your universe
that are even more important
than our happiness or well-being.
The world does not revolve around us,
nor is it designed to satisfy all our
sensual or spiritual appetites.
It seems so natural at times
to make each other
the focal point of our lives,
and then wonder why we are still discontented
and unfulfilled.
You have graciously allowed us to share
our lives with one another,
but never is our happiness
to be an end in itself.
It is a means of beautifying and enriching our lives
in order to make us more fruitful
and effective in our relationships with others.
As our love for each other grows deeper,
make our commitment to you and to other people
more genuine and demonstrative.
We pray that you and your objectives
may always have priority in our lives
and our relationship.

WHEN PRAYING TOGETHER
IS DIFFICULT

We are wondering, our Lord,
why it seems so awkward, at times,
to pray together.
Do we still regard
our individual relationships to you
as something so personal and private?
Or are we drifting away from one another,
assuming that we are
on different wave-lengths
in respect to our faith in you?
We love you,
and we love one another,
and yet it is often difficult
to express ourselves
openly and honestly
in the other's presence.
Grant that we may allow one another
the right to maintain
individual prayer-relationships with you,
even the right to hold back from one another
thoughts and feelings that we believe
to be between each of us and you.
We know our praying together
should be a joyous and enriching experience
that continues to bind us to you
and to one another.
Teach us, our great God,
how to sing and pray and praise you
together.

BREAKING OLD TIES

We are about to move away, Lord,
to pull up deeply embedded roots,
to vacate a friendly environment
and seek out a new place in which to live and work.
There is a measure of excitement
as we anticipate the adventures
of new places and new faces.
There is, as well,
the pain of leaving behind the familiar,
of confining to memory alone
our beautiful experiences and relationships.
Overcome our apprehensions, dear Lord,
and enable us to meet
the challenge before us.
While we express our gratitude
for the friends we have made
and the great times we have had,
help us to assume a place
of responsibility in a new community
and among a new people.
May we never forget, O Lord,
that we are sent by you,
that we are your servants forever,
that you go before us
and will always be with us.
We pray that you will prepare our hearts
for this new arena of service to you
and to our new neighbors for your sake.

CELEBRATING

SHE'S NO ANGEL, LORD

I didn't marry an angel, Lord,
but she's a lot more than I deserve.
She may not measure up
to some of my foolish fantasies,
but she is real and genuine,
a warm body and a loving spirit.
She didn't turn out to be
quite what I expected,
but she is in so many ways
more than I dared to hope.
She doesn't follow my every whim
or discern and meet my every need
or do my every bidding,
but she loves me and sticks by me
in spite of my faults and failings.
She's not perfect, Lord,
though I usually expect more of her
than I do of myself.
But she is my mate, my partner.
She is your gift to me,
and for this I shall be eternally grateful.
Thank you, Lord, for my dear wife.
Help me to be as important to her
as she is to me.

WE'RE STILL MARRIED, THANK GOD

We are still married, our loving Lord,
and we are grateful, to you above all,
and to one another
for the privilege and the pleasure
of these years together.
We know that it is not because of our charm
or ingenuity or determination,
but by your grace
that we are celebrating today.
There have been doubts and dry spells,
disagreements and misunderstandings.
There were even days when we seriously
wondered if it were all worth it.
Whatever the reason, we stayed with it,
even through those rough times
when circumstances about us or within us
sought to drive a wedge between us.
We are grateful, dear God, that through it all
and with your gracious help
we have found a love
that is stronger and richer and more satisfying
than anything for which we dared to hope.
We're still married,
and we thank you, our God.
We shall continue,
in the days or years before us,
to live by your grace
and in obedience to your will.

THE JOY OF RECONCILIATION

Thank you, Lord, for the joy of forgiving
and being forgiven.
Something came between us today.
There were hurt feelings and angry words,
and for several hours we felt
estranged and lonely.
It seems as if everything comes to an end
when our love is smothered
by some silly grievance.
There were moments when we felt
hate toward each other.
We know it is often a projection
of our personal feelings
of inferiority and low worth,
that we are really angry with ourselves
and are stymied because we can't
always have our own way.
As you love us,
even when we foolishly rebel against you,
and reach out to forgive and restore us
to yourself,
so continue to teach us
that love is stronger than hate
and enable us always
to be reconciled to one another.
There is so much happiness
in coming together again.
We thank you for the joy of reconciliation.

THANK GOD
WE'RE DIFFERENT

It may have been our similarities
that brought us together, Lord,
but we are learning how to be grateful
for our differences.
There could hardly be anything quite so dull
as two people who are exactly alike.
We need your help, our God,
to accept each other—
and to respect our differences
and the role they play
in making us what we are,
unique and special and very important
to you and to one another.
While we must tolerate some of the things
we cannot understand in another person,
teach us how to use our differences
to help make up what is lacking in the other.
We thank you, God,
because we are different.
Use our differences,
as well as our similarities,
to enhance and enrich our relationship.

SPATS CAN BE
GOOD SPORT

There was that war of words
again this morning, Lord.
It seems, at times,
that these skirmishes are as much a part
of our relationship
as is our prayer life.
And maybe this is what drives us
to the family altar
to be reconciled to you
and to each other.
We are imperfect, Lord, and failure-fraught.
Is it possible
that even our imperfections are important,
that they serve to keep us open
to your forgiving love
and flowing grace?
Maybe we can be grateful
even for our occasional spats
if they help us to acknowledge our humanity.
Grant, O God,
that they may always keep us close to you,
and make our marriage
a loving and productive relationship.

THANK GOD
FOR OUR MORTGAGED HOME

It means much to us, dear Lord,
to have a place to live—
a place to call our own.
It is a place for our love to grow
and to blossom like the flowers we plant
and the trees that surround our dwelling.
It is a place for us to share with others,
who may find shelter under its roof
and warmth within its rooms.
It is a sanctuary
from the rush of the marketplace
and the noise of busy streets,
a place to live and love and laugh and cry.
It may not be ours for long, O God,
but while you have placed this home
under our stewardship,
we gratefully dedicate it
to you and your purposes
and celebrate the privilege of living
together within its walls.
Forbid, O God, that it become a prison
that confines us to selfish living,
or an anchor that prevents us from pursuing
your objectives throughout our world.
Make it always a place of prayer,
of rest and renewal,
of preparation for consecrated service
to you and your children.

How delightful it is, our great God,
to gather together the frayed ends
of our lives and our relationship
and focus our attention and concern
on your love and grace,
to declare your worth
and celebrate your presence!
Whether we worship in private or in public,
our worship clears the air
and brings peace back to the soul
and assures us once more that your power
is always available to help us
over the rough spots in the road.
It is in the hour of worship
that we are renewed in our relationship
to you and to each other
and rededicated to your course for our lives.
We sing to your glory, our God,
and shout your praises,
for truly you are a great God
and we are your beloved children.

WHEN THE FAMILY
IS TOGETHER

Whether it be a picnic at the park
or the evening meal in the home,
the gathering of the family should be
a time of celebration,
a religious experience,
with or without sermons or scripture lessons.
We pray that it might be so
with us, our Lord,
that we might find joy as we come together,
that we will bypass any bickering,
overcome our misunderstandings,
and know the inner contentment
of family love and unity.
We all belong to you, O God,
and are members of your divine family.
As we relate to you,
may we relate in love to one another,
that we may gather often as a family
to sing songs of love
and shout our praises to you,
our Lord and our God.

THE JOY OF SERVING

The greatest joy of our lives, O Lord,
is the joy of knowing
that we are your children
and are under your appointment and commission
to carry on your objectives
in our world about us.
Thank you, our God, for the joy of serving,
for the joy of knowing that whereas
we differ and even disagree in some areas
of our relationship,
we can discover unity in your love for us
and in sharing your love with one another
and with those around us
And thank you for the grace,
the gifts and talents
that enable us to serve others.
Our roles as individuals may not be the same,
but our goal is one:
to advance your kingdom,
to communicate your healing touch of love
to those who suffer
and to those who are lonely or lost.
Let our joy show through, O Lord,
and transmit joy to the dull lives
of unhappy people in our path.

VACATION TIME

We are grateful, our loving God,
that we can celebrate together
this place of beauty
and this time of rest and relaxation.
We know you were present with us
in the tensions of the city
and the demands of each working day.
And there was beauty to be found
in busy streets and shopping centers,
the offices and institutions
that seek to supply the needs and wants
of this world's multitudes.
Yet there is no beauty
that matches the breath-taking beauty
and grandeur of this place, O Lord.
We would like to build a shrine here, Lord,
but it would only mar
the majestic works of your hands.
Thus we raise our voices in celebration
and pray that our refreshed spirits will glow
with the love and joy and beauty
we have found together in this place
and may help to bring joy
to the tired and unhappy lives
of our brothers and sisters
back there in the city.

SOMEONE TO COME HOME TO

I thank you, my God,
that I have someone to come home to.
It was lonely out there among the masses.
There were uncountable bodies
walking, running, moving about,
but I found no one who cared about me,
who even knew that I existed.
People said "hello" or "how are you?"
"pardon me" or "thank you."
Sounds were uttered,
complaints made, commands given,
but there was no real love to be found.
I thank you, Lord,
that I have someone to come home to,
someone who loves me,
who truly cares about me.
I can endure the loneliness out there
because love follows me and then draws me
back again to warm embraces and kind thoughts,
to comfort and encouragement.
This enables me to minister to
the bodies and spirits
of those who live and work out there.
I thank you, God,
and I pray that those who are out there
in the world
might also have someone
to come home to.

WONDERING

GROWING OLD TOGETHER

How grateful we are, our Lord,
that we can grow old together!
There is a deep joy and abiding contentment
that we never quite realized
in the early years of our marriage.
There is less tension, less striving.
We are truly happy with one another.
We fit together,
knowing well and accepting fully
the other's strengths and weaknesses.
We thank you, our Lord,
for keeping us through the difficult
years of our marriage,
for patiently teaching us how
to love one another.
We are not yet at the end
of our journey, O God.
There will still be battles to be fought,
wounds to be endured,
victories to be won.
But our faith is stronger now—
and our love deeper—
and we seek to live out each day
together with you.
Stay with us, Lord,
and continue to use us
as we grow old together.

SOMETIMES
WE GET LONELY

Sometimes we get lonely, Lord.
Our children,
at one time so dependent upon us,
do not need us any longer.
They have their own set of responsibilities—
and all the problems that go with them.
We cannot expect to be as important
to them as they were and are to us.
Bless them, Lord, and watch over them.
Now may we,
in our matured love for each other,
and in love exchanged with friends,
discover that fullness of love
which will overcome the emptiness and loneliness
that sometimes overwhelms us.
We thank you, God, for what our children
have meant and do mean to us.
Be with us in our absence from them.
Keep us busy with your purposes
and in sharing our love
with other lonely people
who come our way.

WHEN ONE OF US
IS GONE

Because of your love and grace, O God,
we no longer fear the inevitable—
that day and that hour
when we shall part company
with this world's pains and pleasures
to step into your perfect and total
dimension for us.
We belong to you,
and no one or nothing can separate us
from your eternal love. ·
There is something we do dread, O Lord.
It is that one of us will go before the other
and that one will be left alone.
We have become so close
through our many years together
that it is difficult to contemplate
how we could possibly exist
apart from the other.
We are grateful for our years together,
the hours of struggle and defeat
as well as the times of joy and victory.
Teach us how to relish and use to the utmost
every day of our remaining years together.
Give to us the assurance, our God,
that your grace will continue to comfort
and sustain that one who is left behind
when one of us is gone.

GREETING EACH DAY
IN JOY

We may not be able to meet each day
in good health, our Lord,
but we can greet each day in joy.
You have cancelled out our past failures;
you love us even in our weaknesses.
We praise you for your goodness
toward us these many years,
your guarantee of life everlasting
in that eternal and glorious dimension
beyond our own.
We can do no less, Lord,
than to live each day to the full,
to entrust ourselves totally to your mercy
and to express our joy
in loving relationships
with those around us.
May the fire of your Spirit burn brightly
within us, Lord,
and may it cast light
on the dark and lonely paths of others
who come our way.

MORE TIME TO PRAY

We have more time to pray now, Lord,
for our dear children and their families,
for our friends,
many who are ill or lonely,
for your oppressed and suffering children
throughout our world,
for those servants who seek to relate them
to your love and care.
We may not be able to be on the front lines,
but we can and we do unite with those
who continue to demonstrate their concern
for the multitudes
that have not yet embraced your redeeming love.
Grant those who labor in our world
great joy and much power
as they reach out to communicate
your love and grace
to people about them.
Continue to show us
ways in which we might serve you
in the days or years
we have before us.

THOSE BONUS YEARS

We thank you, our God,
for these bonus years
that you have added
to our full and active lives together.
Now we can do some of the things
we have always wanted
but never had the time to do.
We seek to do those things, our Lord,
not only for our pleasure,
but for your service.
We have letters to write,
people to see,
old friends to contact,
ill and lonely people to comfort and cheer.
We thank you for whatever good health remains
and for your grace and strength to enable us
to carry out these projects.
Help us, our great God,
to use these days and years well,
to discover that our greatest joy
does not come in what we do for ourselves
but in what we do for others;
and even as we give of ourselves
to the needs of others,
help us to discover pleasure and fulfillment
in these bonus years before us.

WE ARE ALWAYS
YOUR SERVANTS

We may not be able to serve you
with the energy and aggressiveness
of our youth, our loving God,
nor can we fill those positions of responsibility
you once assigned to us,
but help us to understand and to rejoice in
the fact that we are always your servants.
Your commission is ever before us.
Our appointment as your servants,
will never be rescinded.
Your power is constantly available.
And we are yours forever.
We may be serving in smaller arenas,
but the joy of serving
is as great as ever, O God.
We are as important to you
as we have ever been.
Assure us of our significance
as your servants, O Lord,
and keep reminding us that, wherever we are,
there are people whom we can reach
on your behalf,
to whom we can proclaim
and demonstrate your love.
Empower us, guide us,
work out your will through us,
for we are always your servants.

ARE WE DOING ENOUGH?

We feel guilty, Lord,
in a world so full of pain.
While many of our brothers and sisters
are deprived and oppressed,
we are comparatively happy and secure.
We are concerned, our God,
and we do try to reach out to others in need,
but we are afraid that we are not doing enough.
There is much we cannot do;
there are so many needy people that we cannot reach.
We don't want to feel guilty, Lord.
We need to be assured that we are doing
everything we can
with the gifts you have placed in our hands
and that you forgive us when we fail.
We pray that you will help us
to love others
and to grow in our commitment to you
and your objectives in this arena of service
in which you have placed us.
And we pray for all others
through whom you are working
to care for the suffering multitudes.
Grant, O God, that we, by your grace,
will do all that you
have empowered and equipped us to do.

FAITH
IN A DISSOLVING WORLD

It is difficult, our loving God,
to demonstrate our joy and reflect your love
in a world that is falling apart.
Hatred and violence, dishonesty and disorder,
immorality and lawlessness run rampant
in this beautiful world you created.
Hopelessness and despair haunt
the hearts of men and women.
While frightened people scurry about
for a place to hide
or concoct foolish gods to succor and sustain them,
we turn to you.
You are our Lord and our God.
We believe you to be present in our world
even when you seem to be so far away.
While we grasp for some sign of your presence,
some evidence of your reign over the universe,
teach us how to trust you through the Christ
who has revealed you to us,
to continue to communicate your saving love
amid the hopelessness and despair
of a dissolving world.
And help us to believe that you are here
and through us are accomplishing
your purposes in our world today.
Strengthen and sustain our faith, O God,
that we might walk in obedience to you.